ROADRUNNER !

(and his cuckoo cousins)

Virginia Douglas

Naturegraph

Library of Congress Cataloging in Publication Data
Douglas, Virgina, 1918—
    Roadrunner! : (and his cuckoo cousins)

    Bibliography: p.
    1. Cuckoos.   I. Title.
QL696.C83D68   1984   598'.74   84-982

ISBN 0-87961-147-2

SPECIAL ACKNOWLEDGEMENT

    I am most grateful for permission given by the renowned artist, Delmer J. Yoakum, National Watercolor Society, to use two of his roadrunner paintings for the book's cover. They capture the beauty and appeal of this unique bird.

    Cover paintings and chapter illustrations are by Delmer Yoakum, N.W.S., courtesy of Masters Gallery, Sedona, Arizona.

Books for a better world

Naturegraph Publishers, Inc.
P. O. Box 1075
Happy Camp, California 96039

The roadrunner runs in the road,
His coat, speckled a'la mode.
His wings are short, his tail is long,
He jerks it as he runs along.
His bill is sharp, his eyes are keen,
He has a brain tucked in his bean.
But in his gizzard—if you please—
Are lizards, rats, and bumblebees;
Also horned toads—on them he feeds—
And rattlesnakes! and centipedes!

Eve Ganson
"Desert Mavericks"

TABLE OF CONTENTS

FOREWORD

There is probably no more appropriate symbol of the southwestern United States than the roadrunner or ground cuckoo. It is active in the daylight hours so that anyone can observe it, and it does such strange things! One of the first birds that any foreign visitor wants to see is the famous road-runner. Virginia Douglas has lived in a marvelous area to observe these cuckoos, and when they showed up in her yard she had the curiosity to begin studying them. To learn more, she spent years researching the literature and putting together this interesting account.

She has done a delightful job of chronicling the life of "Ruby" and other roadrunners. Virginia Douglas shows what one can accomplish by taking careful, detailed notes on our birds: times of arrival, singing periods, food, care of young, interaction with other species, etc. This teaches us powers of observation and cognizance of detail. Even if one doesn't write a book about a species of bird, one can contribute such records to ornithological organizations or museums. There is much to be learned about our birds. I know that the reader will enjoy the crazy doings of this bird that can bring smiles to anyone's life.

Bruce J. Hayward
Professor of Biological Science
Western New Mexico University
Silver City, New Mexico

ACKNOWLEDGEMENTS

I wish to thank the following persons for their kind assistance: Dr. Donald Brown, University of California, for reading and criticism of the manuscript and for suggestions on sources of material; the late Bud DeWald, editor, *Arizona Magazine*, for permission to use my story, "A Run of Road-runners," which appeared in that publication; Gary Michael Avery, editor, for permission to use material by the late J. Frank Dobie in *Arizona Highways*; the librarians and staff of Arizona State University Library and the Prescott and Payson Arizona Public Libraries.

Thanks are also due to the National Park Service for presentation of the film, *Life in Parched Lands*, in which is recorded the victory of the roadrunner in a spectacular battle with a desert rattlesnake.

Thanks also to Fred Snyder of Sedona, Arizona, for his interesting roadrunner account.

Special thanks go to Dr. Bruce Hayward, Professor of Biological Sciences, Western New Mexico University, who took the time to critique the manuscript for errors of presentation and ornithology and who wrote the Foreword.

And my husband, Doug, whose career has been with the United States Forest Service, and who shared with me the years of observation and friendship with roadrunners while he recorded on film their lives and antics.

Finally, I wish to acknowledge the friendly and helpful advice provided by Kim Meilicke, editor of Naturegraph. Her perceptive suggestions have done much to improve the final text of this book.

Chapter One
RATTLESNAKE EATER

What bird races freight trains and cars? What bird, dead or alive, brings luck to Indian tribes and inspires legends and ceremonies? What bird challenges vipers and fights them to death? What bird will live in a busy telephone booth, or eat bacon and eggs for breakfast?

In the early days of California and the Southwest, the pioneers often saw a strange bird racing freight wagons and stage coaches along the dusty roads. They called him *Roadrunner*, and he was still at it when automobiles appeared on the scene. He challenged the horseless carriages, speeding ahead of them, then dodging into the brush at the last moment as the cars bore down. Goggle-eyed travelers placed bets on just how fast the bird could run, some wagering at least fifty miles per hour, but when clocked by speedometers over any great distance, the speed dwindled to twelve or fifteen. Though a good horse can outrun him on a straight-away, his agility and speed for short spurts and ziz-zags are unbeatable.

The roadrunner is a symbol of the Southwest. New Mexico has honored him by making him the State bird; the Texas Folklore Society has adopted him as its emblem. Trading posts, stores and highway stands carry his pictures and articles of clothing emblazoned with his profile. While authorities once placed bounties on his head, thinking this clever and beneficial bird to be not only stupid but a ruthless killer of wildlife, new laws and strong public sentiment now protect him.

American Indians and Mexican paisanos have traditionally held the roadrunner in high regard and respected him as a sign of good luck. Plains Indians hung the whole skin of a roadrunner over the lodge door to keep out evil spirits. The Pueblo Indians of New Mexico gave special religious significance to the bird. His tracks, resembling a Maltese Cross, with two toes forward and two toes backward, were duplicated by mourners on the ground around a dead body in order to mislead any evil spirits that might try to follow the departed soul. An Indian mother tied bright roadrunner feathers on the cradleboard to ward off demons that could trouble her child's mind. At least one tribe of California Indians used roadrunner feathers to adorn their headdresses for protection.

South of the Mexican border, natives traveling the mountains believe the *Corredor camino* (runner of the road) to be a guide for all mankind. If a man is lost, he need only follow a roadrunner and it will lead him to a trail. The bird not only fancies trails for travel but apparently follows them to devour the tumble-bug beetles and other insects that feed on the droppings of horses and burros. Mexico loves its cockfights and some devotees boast that their favorite fighters were bred from hens crossed with roadrunners. The ultimate Mexican tribute to the bird, however, is this: folklore insists that it is not the stork that brings babies, but the roadrunner!

The very virtues of the bird may prove his downfall in some areas of Mexico. The Tarahumara Indians of the Sierra Madre, the world's most remarkable runners, regard the flesh of the roadrunner as not only wholesome but conducive to speed and endurance. And a *sure cure* for itch or boils, known all over Mexico and the Southwest, is the eating of fried roadrunner.

Lest we conclude that the Mexican attitude is entirely adulatory, we should record an ancient South-of-the-Border legend: "The roadrunner was once known as the royal pheasant (*Faisan real*), who flew about with eagles and cardinals while scorning the common sparrows, wrens and doves. But one day when the King Eagle was conducting court business with high officials and nobles, the conceited royal pheasant barged, unannounced, into the assembly. The enraged King Eagle ordered the roadrunner to never again claim to be a flying pheasant but to stay on the ground and feed off of beetles, scorpions and tarantulas. When the roadrunner attempted to fly from the royal courtroom, he found that his wings failed him, and he ran ignominiously away like a hen, remaining on the ground ever since."[1]

Doubtless, the most fascinating roadrunner traditions and legends relate to the killing of snakes, notably that much feared western reptile, the rattlesnake. Some of these stories may raise a doubtful eyebrow, but an abundance of scientific evidence and careful observation prove, beyond doubt, that roadrunners not only kill rattlesnakes but do so with great skill and determination. There appear to be two methods by which the bird kills rattlers. The first method, and thoroughly authenticated, is by direct attack, whereby the roadrunner rushes at the snake, feinting and kicking up dust until the snake strikes. The bird then dodges, turns and delivers continuous lightning pecks at the rattler's head until death consumes the deadly reptile. Using the second method, the roadrunner corrals the snake with a barrier of cholla or prickly pear cactus joints, which impale the snake when it tries to escape from this clever assault.

Park rangers at Organ Pipe National Monument in southern Arizona have featured a motion picture film–lecture demonstrating the direct-attack method. The bird versus rattlesnake combat scenes show the remarkable quickness and agility of the roadrunner as it avoids repeated strikes by the rattlesnake, much as a mongoose baffles a cobra.

Difficult to deny its plausibility, the cactus corral technique for rattler kills has been described by many types of observers at different times and from separate geographic areas of the United States and Mexico. The accounts, however, are typically by hunters and ranchers, rather than by biologists. In Texas, for example, quail hunters stumbled across a brutal battle scene. The roadrunner, holding a cactus pad, shielded himself from the rattler, already pierced by numerous prickly pear thorns. After the snake continued to strike several times at the pad, the roadrunner discarded it and ran to fetch another. In time, the snake, exhausted and covered with thorns, no longer struck its victorious opponent.

On another occasion, a pair of Texas miners cited a rattlesnake sunning itself near the entrance to their mine tunnel. Two roadrunners, who were in the habit of visiting their camp daily, spied the snake and immediately proceeded to make a small corral of cholla joints. They worked quietly until the crude circle grew to about three inches in height. When they ran at the snake, uttering sharp cries, the reptile awoke, struck out instantly and transfixed itself on the sharp cholla thorns. The more it twisted and turned, the deeper the spines penetrated the underside of the neck. In less than half an hour the writhing snake lay still and the roadrunners proceeded to hack off pieces of meat to feed to their young.

In Sonora, Mexico, an Opata Indian watched a roadrunner build a four-inch cholla cactus wall around a coiled, sleeping rattler. Then the bird leaped upon a rock and dropped a cactus joint squarely on top of the sleeping rattler. Frantic, the snake slashed against the enclosure, perforating itself. Losing all defenses, the prostrated snake fell prey to the roadrunner, who attacked and killed it. Celebrating its victory, the roadrunner sampled the rattlesnake by swallowing the head first. Then, retiring to a secluded spot, the champion took hours to digest its victim.

While out with his dogs, a Texas hunter came across a roadrunner with a snake dangling from its mouth. The bird kept tripping over the reptile in its efforts to escape the pursuing dogs, and when it entangled itself and the snake in some brush, the dogs killed it. Pulling the snake out, the hunter found it to be two feet in length. Other observers runners swallowing rattlers three or more feet in length.

It would be surprising if rattlers never succeeded in striking their attackers, but biologists have not reported such. One would suppose that a strike would be fatal to a bird, though if we can credit a Mexican tradition, the bird is smart enough, after being struck, to seek out and eat a celebrated herbal snakebite cure called *huaco*. Natives in San Luis Potosi and elsewhere declare that they discovered its value by witnessing stricken roadrunners eating it.

Why do people with such eagerness watch, study and befriend roadrunners? There is a certain rapport between these birds and humans. In the early 1920s a family building a home at Twenty Nine Palms in the Mojave Desert encountered a roadrunner at their campsite. He would approach slowly, in the early morning, making a clacking noise with his beak. Then he made a regular ritual of sharing breakfast with his hosts, afterwards cleaning up the skillet of bacon bits and scrambled egg and then taking other leftovers from their hands. Another built a nest in their outhouse, and still another accepted a sort of kennel built by the family on a porchbeam. A remarkable feature of the behavior of these and other roadrunners is the regularity of their habits. A bird will establish certain routes, which he covers faithfully at the same time each day. An invalid convalescing on the Colorado desert noted that one bird passed her porch on his rounds at exactly 12:25 p.m. daily. A rancher building a new fence around his desert home observed that a roadrunner seemed to be so intrigued with the structure that it would spring up onto the top rail and then run full speed down the entire length of one side—at twelve noon daily.

A pair of roadrunners used to call regularly at a ranch near Santa Fe, New Mexico, just in time for the feeding of cracked corn to the chickens and then would often roost with them at night. Another pair came every day at the same hour to a mining area near Hachita for water. A foxhound belonging to one of the mine workers would watch eagerly for their arrival and then give chase as soon as he sighted them. The birds seemed delighted with this game and had no difficulty keeping out of the dog's way and still managing to get their fill of water. After satisfying their thirst and tiring of the sport, they ran off into the brush while the dog returned to his usual spot on the doorstep.

Finally, there is the case of the roadrunner at Quartzsite in the western Arizona desert. This character decided to take up residence in a roadside telephone booth, where local residents enjoyed stroking his head as they made their calls. Eventually, he consented to make his home with a gentleman who lived alone nearby. Having the run of the house, the bird perched here and there on the furniture, but returned to sleep in the telephone booth at night for several months before deciding to make the man's cabin his permanent abode.

And so lives the amazing roadrunner. In Texas they call him *Chapparal Cock*; in New Mexico, *Lizard Eater* or *Snake Eater*. Arizonans call him all three. They know him in Mexico as *Paisano* (countryman), or along the Rio Grande as *Churilla* (grouse), and in Sonora as *Faisan* (pheasant). By whatever name, he remains the same bird, the California roadrunner, a ground cuckoo, *Geococcyx californanus*.

Chapter Two
HABITS AND HABITAT

Who is this strange desert denizen who not only tackles deadly reptiles but finds recreation in chasing golf balls on the fairways or in pursuing the dragging chains of surveyors? Let me try to describe him and his habitat, his diet, his mating, nesting and parenting methods, and his enemies. But always keep in mind that the roadrunner is such a confirmed individualist that exceptions may be found to almost anything you say about him.

The Bird

Before you ever see a roadrunner you may hear its almost alarming, incisive clackety voice made by rolling the mandibles together rapidly. Or you may hear a cackling and cooing sound, used to attract mates or to call the young chicks, who in turn, make a buzzing sound as they call for food. If you are patient, you may discover a large bird emerging from the brush, measuring from twenty to twenty-four inches in length, with a foot long tail and short wings. The legs are long and the feet are large with two of the four toes facing backwards, the outer back toe being reversible to aid in climbing and perching. The long, sharp, slightly curved beak is very strong, and it can snap through a scorpion or tarantula like a pair of shears.

If the roadrunner comes close, you will see his upper parts conspicuously streaked brown and white. His high crest (which he raises and lowers at will) and foreparts are black, glossed with steel-blue and shaded to a bronzy-green on the lower back. The upper and middle tail feathers are an olive-bronze that also shine with purple, while the outermost blue-black and green feathers are tipped with white thumb marks. The underparts are a plain gray. The light yellow or cream scales of the leg are margined with blue. The bright eyes, so alert and mischievous, will grab your attention. The iris is golden yellow surrounded by blue skin in front, blending into bluish-white, and in back of the eye flashes a brilliant orange-red patch.

Underneath the feathers, a coarse furlike down enables the roadrunner to endure snow and cold weather. When animated or alarmed, the feathers press close to the body, the neck extends in the direction of flight, the headcrest rises to full height, and the vivid colors behind the eyes gleam in a band about the head. The roadrunner's strong legs flee from danger, and only if pressed or startled does it take wing, gliding for short distances with comparative ease and swiftness. An eyewitness describes the volplaning flight: "It merely pitched off with head, wings and tail outstretched from a cliff, fifty feet high, and glided down a canyon an eighth of a mile in the most gentle and graceful undulations, never flapping a wing once, not even when it alighted upon a rock, where it closed its wings, raised its head and looked around with great unconcern."[1]

On cold days you may see the roadrunner sunning himself in the warm early morning rays. With his back to the sun, he holds out his wings and fluffs out his feathers, revealing an area of dark-colored skin that absorbs heat and raises the bird's temperature. This is essential since an internal thermostat permits the body's temperature at night to drop some seven degrees below daytime normals. On the other hand, the roadrunner can stand terrific heat. During the desert summer, you may observe him standing with open beak and panting like a dog, though during the hottest daylight hours he will seek shade in trees or brush.

Since roadrunners prosper in arid deserts, far from water, some ornithologists believe that water is not essential to survival. This may well be true in areas where the birds have adapted themselves to such conditions and can obtain foods containing a high percentage of fluid, but if water is available they will drink often and long. A roadrunner cannot swim and many have lost their lives by drowning in stock tanks and open cisterns, especially when the water level has evaporated to a level too low for them to reach without falling in. Some ranchers provide wood floats for birds to use when drinking in deep, open water tanks.

One final note on the bird and its habits concerns that crazy, foot-long tail! Like a feathered hammer driving invisible nails into the desert earth, that tail seldom stops pumping up and down no matter where the bird ventures.

The Environment

You probably saw, or will see, your first roadrunner somewhere in the scrub desert of the lowlands and valley floors of the Southwest between Texas and Southern California. Here, the plants, three to six feet high, are widely spaced. Creosote bush (*Larrea*) is often the dominant plant, but other common plants include mesquite (*Prosopis*), palo-verde (*Cercidium*), catclaw (*Acacia*), ironwood (*Olneya*), ocotillo (*Fouquieria*), agaves, cacti, and yuccas. The roadrunner scampers through the lower Sonoran and the lower part of the Upper Sonoran zones in California, Arizona, Utah, Colorado, New Mexico, Kansas, Oklahoma, and western and middle Texas, south through lower California and the tablelands of Mexico, as far as Puebla.

The *chapparal cock* also makes his home in a wide range of elevations, from sea level on the Pacific Coast of Mexico and California and the Mexican Gulf Coast beyond Tampico to 7500 feet in the inland mountains of its habitat. In the heart of its range, West Texas, New Mexico, and Arizona, the bird frequently appears in all the valleys below 5000 feet, especially in those east of the Rio Grande. Just to prove that the roadrunner can defy any general statement made about him, we may cite the remarkable discovery in 1907 of a specimen at Marshall Pass, Colorado, at an elevation of 10,000 feet! Except in the extreme northern parts of its range, the bird resides and breeds wherever found. Once he chooses a home, he seldom leaves the vicinity and may be found there year after year. In Texas, however, there has been some question as to migration, since more roadrunners appear in summer than during the winter months. On one ranch a bird would leave each fall and then reappear every spring. In any case, the runners I have observed in Arizona "stay home" throughout the four seasons.

The Diet

How much food and of what variety does it take to satisfy this feathered paisano that weighs only about a pound? Quite a lot, it would seem, and of an incredible variety. He has an appetite as queer as his looks. He swallows horned toads, grasshoppers, moths, centipedes, scorpions, millepedes, tarantulas, cutworms, spiders, bumblebees, mice, rats, young rabbits, and snakes. He will occasionally eat birds' eggs and small birds. He savors such vegetable foods as prickly pear cactus fruits and sumac berries. But the roadrunner delights chiefly in lizards, which are, at times, his main fare. No matter how fast a lizard darts and dodges, the bird rarely fails to follow and seize and then dispatch this prey with a single blow of his powerful beak. One of the commonest sights in roadrunner country is to see the bird standing or running with a lizard dangling from his mouth.

There are endless accounts of the paisano's strange eating habits. He flies into chicken pens and eats the henscratch. He consumes breadcrumbs and watermelon. One observor watched a roadrunner turn over dozens of cakes of mud in a desert dry-lake bed. These cakes were seven or eight inches across, nearly an inch thick, and very heavy. Small, grey-black crickets were under each upturned block, and the bird was devouring them. In southwest Texas, a runner, observed picking up snails, broke the shells on a special rock he had appeared to select as a meat-block, and then indulged in the meat. In severe winters, the bird will even resort to the eating of carrion if hard-pressed for food.

Thus, the roadrunner is a part of the intricate chain of life on the desert. It begins with such plants as *Schismus barbatus* grass that produces food starch from sunlight, air and water. Small animals, and insects like the cricket, eat the grass, and in turn, they are eaten by desert animals, such as the spiny lizard. A snake comes along and eats the lizard and then a hungry roadrunner catches and eats the snake. Finally, a ringtail cat may seize and eat the roadrunner.

Courtship and Mating

When a male roadrunner stakes out a territory, advertising his presence with a song consisting of a series of coos descending in scale, courtship begins. The female answers and slowly arrives in sight of the cooing male. The male stamps his feet, bowing and cackling rapidly, and repeats the whole performance until she accepts him, which may take quite some time to achieve. I have often seen the male follow the female about for several days offering bits of grass, an insect, or a small twig. He continues to coo to the female, who may ignore him or run away. But gradually the female begins to tolerate the male's presence and eventually she even accepts his gift. Then they chase each other around the brush and into the trees with much cooing and cackling. The male holds his head high and raises his crest to full height with all his vivid colors showing.

Having had roadrunners as pets in our family, I have had the interesting opportunity to witness courtship maneuvers, discovering the promiscuity of the male bird. I vividly recall the time a male approached both our female roadrunners with various gifts, but then followed the female he found most receptive. Later the other female reappeared with two chicks following her and we assumed the male was the father.

Nesting

You will be lucky if you ever find a roadrunner's nest, as the immense mess of sticks and trash blends with the brush and scrub so well as to be almost invisible except at close range. The bird tramples the structure down in the middle and lines it with snake skins, feathers, rootlets, catkins, or any fine material available. Sometimes roadrunners, accustomed to the presence of humans, may nest in a barn, ranch outbuilding or an abandoned desert shack. But ordinarily, the bird nests in mesquite, paloverde, juniper, sycamore trees, or cactus clumps, and occasionally chooses the abandoned nest of some other large bird.

The nesting season usually begins in the latter part of March or early April, but can be as late as mid-May. The bird lays her eggs at considerable intervals and incubation begins as soon as the first egg arrives. Hatching takes eighteen days for each, requiring the patient mother to sit almost seven weeks on the nest, first with the eggs and then with the young. It isn't that the period of incubation is so unusually long or that the young birds are slow in growing, but rather that their method of hatching enables the first fledgling to fly from the nest by the time the last chick breaks through its shell. After the second or third bird hatches, the body heat of the young suffices to keep the remainder of the eggs warm.

Eggs are chalky-white, pure white, or yellowish in color. The average clutch is four to six, although two to three eggs often comprise a set, and eight are not uncommon, with records of up to twelve eggs. When such a large number occur in one nest, it is likely more than one female has deposited them.

Does the hen do all the work? Hatching takes place at the height of the food supply cycle, when food can be found over an extended period of time. The spacing of chicks would suggest that the female does all the brooding and feeding, on the theory that, since chicks do not hatch at the same time, the mother need only feed those already hatched. However, biologists have observed both parents apparently taking turns in minding the nest and hunting food. Judging from my personal experience, I would have to doubt that the male helps with incubation and feeding, except, perhaps, rarely. I have seen males approach the female during nesting time, only to be greeted with a deep, guttural sound of anger. The female's crest erected to its full height and she appeared ready to fight or flee. Under these circumstances, the males usually retreated.

If humans approach the female roadrunner while nesting, she generally remains quiet until the intruder is nearly upon her. Should incubation be well advanced, the female will sometimes allow herself to be caught on the nest, rather than abandon her eggs or young. Otherwise she slips over the back of the nest and flies a short distance away where she can still see the unwelcome caller. One observer reported seeing a roadrunner hop to the ground, squirm, scramble, and drag herself across an open space, away from the nest, and in full view of the intruder. The bird was simulating a broken leg, instead of a broken wing! She did this until about thirty-five feet away and then immediately returned to the base of the nest tree and repeated the whole performance. The bird continued this stunt until she reached a point well outside the grove of sycamores where she was nesting, and then suddenly ran full speed, still farther from the nest.

The Young

The newly-hatched roadrunner's coarse, long, white plumage does not cover its dark-skinned body, yet provides all the protection the bird requires. Large, pale, blue-gray feet feature strong toes which enable the birds to cling to twigs of their nest with some power. However their weak heels prevent them from rising. The young are able to run well, but remain in trees like young green herons who spend a portion of their early active life climbing about from branch to branch.

At this infant stage, the light-colored egg tooth (a hard tip on the end of the beak used to break through the shell) is still noticeable, the mouth lining has a blotched appearance and the irises are dull brown. Later, as blood quills replace the long white hairs, the egg tooth disappears, the skin about the back of the eye lightens, and the blotching of the mouth lining becomes less conspicuous. The sprouting feathers bear at their tips the white hairs of babyhood. Some of these hairs cling to the plumage long after the bird leaves the nest.

The chief difference in color, as compared to adults, consists in the broad shaft stripes of the neck and breast feathers which are less sharply defined in the young. Soon the bare skin about the eye becomes light blue, and the naked patching back of the eye, light orange. The eye itself changes to a light-colored ring, which contrasts sharply with the brown or gray-brown of the rest of the iris forming about the pupil. As the bird matures, the bare skin of the face brightens. Full adult males, at the height of the breeding season, sparkle with high blue crests, brilliant eyes, and bright orange or red patches in back of the eyes.

Roadrunner mothers eventually brought their fledglings with them when they approached me to beg for handouts. Nearly grown, their bodies large as adults and fully feathered with shiny new plumage, they were obviously still young birds, following their mothers about, whining to be fed, and vying for attention. They squatted, fluttered their wings and made buzzing sounds, features characteristic of other baby birds, such as finches, sparrows, towhees, cardinals, and orioles. When their mothers became busy elsewhere, the chicks' sense of adventure and curiosity kept them amused. At our own home, I marvelled over their games of tag and snapping up food without waiting for their parents to fetch it for them. At one time, three chicks thoroughly inspected our Ford pickup. At first, I wondered when their mothers would teach them caution, a trait that characterizes the roadrunner. Just as I thought these chicks, unafraid of humans, could readily be tamed, their mothers approached to scold and chase their fledglings back into the brush, obviously aware that they were getting too close to me.

Enemies

The bobcat, ring-tailed cat, and domestic and feral cats take a great toll of fledgling roadrunners. Large hawks, and occasionally eagles, cause some loss to adult birds. I have watched them run for cover, along with quail and other birds, when hawks were spotted in the sky. But the paisano's worst enemy remains man, who for years tried unsuccessfully to exterminate him. Even now, despite protective laws, the youngster with a .22 caliber rifle finds the chapparal cock an all too tempting target.

The roadrunner is no coward. When attacked he may himself become the aggressor, as a pair of marsh hawks learned when they chased a paisano into the shelter of a creosote bush. The hawks alighted on the ground and made repeated dives into the foliage. The roadrunner did not remain hidden for long, but suddenly came out fighting. The hawks, out of their element, dashed awkwardly around the bush while the roadrunner kept after them in hot pursuit, until finally the hawks gave up and flew off. Triumphant, the roadrunner, head held high and rattling his beak, ran off at top speed.

Chapter Three
RUBY – AND A FEW OTHERS

When my husband and I bought a piece of desert land on Tonto Creek, south of Payson, Arizona, we believed we had clear title to the property. Although the deed so declared, we discovered that the place was still owned by some road-runners. Not long after we began cutting brush and digging out rocks, several runners came dashing across *our* property, where they stood watching us with apparent indignation, or, perhaps, just curiosity.

This continued until one day we noticed a young female, sleek, trim, and full of life, who came up behind us as we worked, announcing her presence with a loud clacking—a sound similar to castanets. In the open, switching her long tail from side to side and shuffling her feet, she seemed to delight in startling us. Her crest shot up and down, showing off her blue and white colors in addition to a gorgeous deep red, which is why we named her Ruby.

I'll never forget how she actually followed us up the path to our trailer, only a week later, when we broke off work for lunch. We grabbed a bit of hamburger and tossed it to her. She caught it in midair, swallowed it, and stood waiting for more. We threw her other tidbits, some of which she missed and allowed to fall in the sand. Nonetheless, Ruby picked up the hamburger pieces and shook them vigorously to remove the dirt before eating. Since our first experience feeding Ruby hamburger, this remained her favorite food.

We built Ruby a low table of flat rocks, which she attended each afternoon, clacking for her dinner. When our supply of hamburger ran out, she ate liver, suet or lunchmeat. As she became tamer, I coaxed her to take food from my hand, which she finally did, on her own terms, sometimes taking an entire meal from my fingers, at other times only a bite. Always wary, she would dash off a few feet to consume her food. Still, even after three years of close association, she doesn't trust me completely, and I have never been able to touch her.

An assortment of lizards is Ruby's chosen delicacy. Using her sharp beak, she digs them out of the walls, chases them up and down tree trunks and pursues them over open ground. When she captures one, she stands a moment with the victim dangling from her mouth, a gleam of triumph in her sharp black eyes. Then she swallows it whole in a gulp. In addition, she loves grasshoppers and small white moths, seldom allowing anything to escape. Through the coveys of quail so prevalent here, she struts back and forth to show her authority, sometimes scattering them, but I have never seen her really attack or injure adults or chicks.

The wind and rain Ruby could easily live without. The wind catches her tail feathers and sometimes capsizes her. If a shower surprises her, she finds shelter under our pickup and waits dejectedly, feathers fluffed and head withdrawn, until the rain stiops. She drinks from the birdbath, but never bathes in anything but dust or ashes. Wood ashes apparently rid her of bird mites.

Like other roadrunners, Ruby's large bump of curiosity leads her to examine the wheelbarrow, a roll of fencing or some new object she finds in the yard. She investigates any strange car parked in our area, strutting in front of the chrome hubcaps and inspecting the windshield and radiator for insects. She even perches on rearview mirrors and peers in the windows. One day when the electric meter reader drove up and left his car door open, Ruby hopped onto the seat and thoroughly inspected the inside.

Throughout our first year's winter months and into spring, Ruby visited daily, usually in early morning or late afternoon. Sometimes she would miss a day, even two, but after one of her absences, she was always full of talk, as though to bring us up-to-date on her activities. Once she failed to return, and we became concerned. Had she grown tired of our company, found new friends?

It was ten days before we heard the familiar clacking and hurried out. Ruby, on her table, waited to be fed. With dull bedraggled feathers and a small perforation on her breast with frayed down around it, she was a sorry sight. Her right leg was tucked against her body, the foot useless, and dried blood and swelling surrounded the leg and foot joint.

Ruby must have remained hidden until hunger drove her to us. She gulped down a big meal of hamburger, then hopped off slowly in her usual direction. Had someone taken a shot at her, or a hawk swooped down? Had she flown into barbed wire? We could only speculate, as she would not permit us to get close enough to determine the extent of her wounds. Each day she hopped in on her good leg to be fed, and after a week she touched the injured foot to the ground. At the end of two weeks, she was limping on it, and in a month, she appeared healed.

That June we left Tonto Creek for a month's vacation. While we were gone, we often wondered how Ruby was. Upon our return, we watched but saw nothing of her for three long weeks. We missed her proud strut and familiar presence. Then one morning Ruby arrived clacking insistently. I hurried to feed her, but instead of swallowing the hamburger balls, she took three in her beak and ran off. In twenty minutes she returned clacking for more. She kept this up for some twenty trips throughout the day. Finally in the evening, she ate her share of hamburger and carried none away.

Ruby repeated the performance in the days that followed, carrying the food to her hidden brood. Several times I trailed her. I knew that in this kind of habitat roadrunners build their nests seven to ten feet up in juniper or sycamore trees, but no matter where I looked, I never found the nest or saw any of her young.

After two weeks, Ruby did not return as often, though we could hear her in or near our property softly clacking all day. We had thought that she would bring her chicks in for us to see and feed, but though I wandered frequently toward the sound of her, she always eluded me, and thus we never glimpsed her babies. She must have decided that her private hamburger dining room was to remain hers alone, as she was apparently teaching her brood to hunt and capture insects.

The following summer we departed for the cooler north country. Absent three months, I worried over Ruby and missed her companionship. Three days after our return home,

Ruby, back on her table, clacked and cackled as though we had never been away. For the third winter we enjoyed her company and antics.

Did other roadrunners see and envy Ruby and decide to get into the act? In any case, one early spring morning, while eating her meal, Ruby's crest raised in alarm, her neck stretched out and she stood at full height. It was a few moments before we spotted another female behind her. With wings spread out, Ruby quickly ran the other female away. Two days later the new one returned. She accepted food from us, and Ruby, cackling in protest, let us know she felt betrayed.

Perhaps to avoid Ruby, the new female chose a different time to beg. Not the lady that Ruby was, she ate as much as we fed her, then perched on our steps for nearly a half hour, hoping for more. In a squatting position, she moved in closer and closer, easing forward with jerks and small grunts. We called her Rachel. She began to dominate Ruby, absconding with her food. A true glutton, Rachel also called on neighbors for treats.

One May afternoon, a large male arrived. Ruby and Rachel took off at once while the male stayed in the background appraising the situation. Readily accepting a ball of meat tossed in his direction, he did not approach us but simply kept his distance and caught the morsel on the fly. He was a young bird, fully developed, and we named him Ralph. Unlike the females, he did not join us regularly, although he did our neighbor. Since he squatted and grunted for a time, we were not sure if he were Ralph or Rachel. When he came closer, we could readily tell the difference as he was larger than the females, his beak was thicker and longer, and his feet were huge. Greedy, he also developed the habit of running off, only to return later, as though he were an entirely different bird. Ralph became our next door neighbor's pet. He perched on their deck railing and pecked on the adjacent window to attract their attention. He never missed catching the balls of meat tossed to him no matter from which direction the morsels came.

One morning my husband called for me to come quickly. Ruby trotted up the path with Ralph following her, a twig of hackberry in his beak. As Ruby took her accustomed place, Ralph offered it to her. When she ignored him and ran away, he dropped the twig and ate his meal before departing.

The next day and for several days thereafter, Ralph followed Ruby up the trail with all kinds of offerings, various twigs and even a tuft of grass. By this time, Ruby, not as irritated by his presence, squatted and sometimes accepted his offering. When this occurred, Ralph's crest stood erect and his colors beamed. He wagged his tail, doglike, from side to side and shifted his weight from foot to foot, all the while cooing. As Ralph's dance accelerated, Ruby rose and quickly departed. With Ralph at her heels, they chased each other around the low bushes and in and out of the trees, finally disappearing up the hillside.

Several days went by without Ralph. Then, returning without an offering, he picked up his ball of meat and gave it to Ruby. She accepted it, and Ralph repeated his tail-wagging and cooing. Again Ruby departed. He chased her and once more they played the run-around-the-bushes game. The last time they did this courtship dance, it was more intense than previously, and Ruby cooed in tune with Ralph. The courtship shortly ended, presumably followed by mating. Ruby then resumed her visits as usual and Ralph began calling for his handouts, but his visits no longer coincided with hers. The last time they met, Ruby was feeding. They looked at each other as total strangers, and she relinquished her place at the table to him.

Days later, when Ruby returned, there followed two weeks of frenzied chick feeding. The weather was extremely hot, and thus she began her motherly tasks early in the morning. By noon, she was panting, with wings held away from her body, but never pausing more than a few minutes to rest in the shade. During the long hot afternoons, all was quiet. In early evening the feeding resumed, until just before dark, when she fed herself and disappeared to roost with her brood.

One bright morning Ruby showed up with two juveniles in tow, both larger than herself, boisterous and demanding. She parked them close by, where they squatted, making rasping, throaty noises. With a supply of meat in her beak, she approached one, who fluttered its wings as any baby bird and opened its beak to be fed. The next piece of meat she took to the second chick, and then the chicks began coming to her. When apparently Ruby had had enough, she carried the meat across the road and vanished in the brush, leaving the chicks to chase each other all over the yard and hunt bugs and grasshoppers on their own.

Soon Ruby was able to relax, as her youngsters, more and more, were able to find their own food. She returned regularly as before, to her hamburger table.

Ruby's long intimacy with my husband and me is not a unique experience, and it characterizes the behavior of many of her species. Other first-hand accounts tell of this rapport that the roadrunner has with humans and even with some domestic animals.

A young roadrunner shared a home with a family at Antelope, California. The bird stayed in the house at night but trotted out early in the morning and jumped to the top of a mound of granite boulders nearby. There he would puff out his feathers, spread his wings and lower his tail, the posture he assumed for his daily sunbath. He would next visit a cactus patch and in a succession of leaps, jumps, and runs go round and round twenty or more times, adopting as many clownish poses as possible.

When he later returned to the house, he amused himself by teasing the cat. He would rush toward the feline with spread wings, extended neck, wide-open mouth, and snapping beak, and make a strange rattling sound in his throat. The cat countered this noisy charge with a quick bat of its paw. The bird then retreated and rushed at the cat again. The game ended when the cat ran away with the roadrunner chasing it.

This particular roadrunner loved fuzzy objects and would bring milkweed seeds or wads of cotton into the house. On occasion, he was also known to bring trash and leaves inside. Once he carried in a sizable piece of glass to show his mistress and to her amazement, swallowed it without any apparent ill effects. When she sprinkled the family wash, he enjoyed her dousing him as well. Any loose objects he found on shelves, such as crayons or a vase of flowers, he would toss to the floor. He harassed the neighbor's barefoot children by picking at their toes when they came to visit. If they wore shoes, he untied their laces.

The bird slept inside the house at night, either on a tree branch nailed above the door or on top of a pendulum clock, his tail pushed flat up against the wall. He ignored the striking of the clock, paid no heed to evening conversations and went to sleep with the lights on. One evening when a stranger came and sat down in a chair under the clock, the bird jumped from his perch onto the visitor's head, then down to his lap where he repeatedly pecked at his fingers.

On a summer morning, they found the roadrunner caught in a rabbit trap in the garden. One foot was so nearly severed that amputation was necessary. With only a stump, the bird could no longer leap or run. He spent several days lying in the shade. By the end of that week, he was hobbling around and three days later was leaping up with the aid of his wings to snatch cicadas from the branches of shrubs. Before a month went by, the roadrunner was back to most of his old tricks. The stump of his leg became sore at times from overuse, but after awhile he developed a callus so thick that he was able to resume his familiar antics around the neighborhood.

An even more intimate relationship with humans appears to develop when it begins with the chicks, especially when the human is an eager and curious youth. A boy in Fort Worth, Texas, managed to raise a pair of baby roadrunners and his story is so remarkable that I am quoting portions of the account that he later wrote as a professional ornithologist.

He found a roadrunner nest not far from his home and kept account of the egg laying and hatching of the young birds. When they were fully feathered and fairly well developed but still unable to fend for themselves, he took two of the nestlings home and collected insects to feed them. The young roadrunners eagerly consumed untold numbers of grasshoppers, cave crickets and bugs. After a period of three weeks, they grew sturdy enough to catch some of their own food. With a lot of coaxing, the boy taught them to pick up grasshoppers he tossed in their direction and finally to run after and capture crippled insects.

The food problem was largely solved once the birds could capture prey on their own. Stealing about through the weeds, they snapped up insects as fast as they discovered them. They learned to hunt for their favorite delicacy, gray or cave crickets, in damp places and piles of boards. When yellow or coral-winged grasshoppers rose noisily, the birds at first crouched in momentary fear. It was not long, however, before they began to mark the insects' return to earth and see just where they landed. Darting after them with outspread wings and tails, the birds snapped up the grasshoppers and beat them to insensibility with a whack or two on a stone.

At liberty most of the time and showing no inclination to run away, the roadrunners ran about the yard playing with each other or catching insects. In the heat of mid-day, they sought the shelter of broad, cool leaves. The boy began taking them for daily walks across the prairie. The birds followed closely or ran at his side, and no movement escaped their sharp eyes. They captured insects that flew up ahead of them. When the boy stopped to turn over a flat stone, they urged him on with grunts, bit gently at his hands, and raced back and forth in anticipation. He wondered if young roadrunners could manage swift-tailed scorpions, or poisonous spiders: "Under the first stone were scorpions. The roadrunners hesitated an instant, then rushed forward, thrust out their heads, and attacked the scorpions precisely at their tails. Perhaps these venomous tails received more than the usual number of benumbing blows, but the scorpions were swallowed with gusto."[1]

Next he wondered if his roadrunners were ready to capture and devour a tarantula. One day, discovering the tunnel of one of these black arachnids, the boy teased the big furred spider from her lair by twirling a wisp of grass in her face. "She popped out viciously and jumped a good ten inches to one side. With a dash, one bird was upon the monster before she had the opportunity to leap a second time, and then with a toss of the bird's head, one of the eight legs was gone. Free again, the spider leaped upon her captor. The other bird now entered the combat, snatched up the spider, and flicked off another leg. One by one the legs went down, and finally the two birds pulled apart and gulped the sable torso."[2]

A large cotton rat lived in a stone wall near the house. Several times a day this rodent scurried across a gap in the wall while the birds watched him with interest. His speed and size kept them as mere spectators for a time, but they finally gained enough courage to attempt to capture him. Hearing a frantic squeal one day, the boy rushed out in time to see the frightened rat running desperately back and forth trying to escape two lightning-quick birds. "They pinched him, tossed him, dealt him blows, buffeted him, and made him weary with fighting for life. Over his limp form the roadrunners had an argument. He was heavy. No sooner would one bird start to swallow than the other would be tugging at the hind foot or tail and down he would drop."[3] The argument was settled when the boy cut the rat in two.

Chapter Four
AND HIS CUCKOO COUSINS

As unbelievable as it may seem, an actual forty-five million years ago the roadrunner's relatives, the yellow-billed and black-billed cuckoos, the groove-billed ani, and others migrated from the Old World.

Most cuckoos belong to two subfamilies with their relatives, the roadrunner and ani. One subfamily to which the common cuckoo belongs ranges across the Old World from Western Europe and Africa, across Asia to the Pacific, while the other belongs to both the Old and New Worlds. Thirty-seven species known as *true cuckoos* occur in the Old World, and they thrive chiefly in the African and Indo-Malayan tropics.

These true cuckoos lay their eggs in the nests of other species, leaving the hatching and the care of the young to the host pair. How did this unusual habit originate? Actually the origin of brood parasitism is not known. It may be that the sight of a nest egg resembling her own acts as a stimulus inducing the female to add to the number. However, in the case of the cuckoos, whose victims are not near relatives, the habit may have started from lack of correlation between laying and nest-building. The fact that the habit characterizes so many species of cuckoo, suggests it is a trait of ancient origin. The European cuckoo, *Cuculus canorus*, for instance, parasitizes over 125 species of birds.

At the beginning of the breeding season, the female cuckoo seeks out and intently observes a bird actively building a nest or laying her eggs, and perhaps the sight of such a host stimulates the cuckoo to ripen an egg follicle and lay. The time interval between such a psychic stimulus and the subsequent laying of the egg amounts to four or five days, and this interval corresponds to that in many small birds, between the time of destruction of one clutch of eggs and the laying of the first egg in the replacement clutch.

Cuckoos are highly deceptive and can imitate actions, calls, and even the plumage of other birds. The Old World cuckoo developed brood parasitism to such a degree that it now lays eggs of a color that matches those of the host species, even to the extent of laying a reddish egg to simulate the reddish egg of a warbler. Red eggs are extremely rare.

The cuckoo hatches in about twelve-and-a-half days, whereas the eggs of most host species require thirteen or fourteen days. This gives the young cuckoo the enormous advantage of a head start over its foster brothers and sisters in growth and in claiming food from the host parents.

When the young cuckoo hatches, it faces the world blind and naked. However, it is muscular and able to gape for food like most immature young. When about ten hours old, an instinct appears that is one of the wonders of the animal kingdom. If any solid object, an egg, young bird, or even an acorn, touches a sensitive shallow depression on the little cuckoo's back, the blind bird manipulates the object to the rim of the nest and shoves it overboard. The young cuckoo persists in this behavior until it has cleared the nest of everything but itself. In these particular cuckoos, the shallow pit on the bird's back soon fills in and young cuckoos lose the impulse to eject after a very short time—almost invariably within a week of being hatched. The urge of many parent birds to brood and feed anything within the nest and to ignore anything outside, encourages this murderous instinct of the cuckoo.

As the cuckoos migrated across the ocean to the Americas, they abandoned, for the most part, the parasitic habits of Old World relatives, building their own nests and raising their own young in the conventional manner. However, some American cuckoos are careless about laying eggs in each others nests where ranges overlap. They have also been known to lay in nests of robins and catbirds, and there are records of the wood-thrush, cedar waxwing and cardinal being imposed upon. These occurrences appear to be rare and may be due to accidents when the birds' own nests have been capsized and necessity compels the deposit of the eggs elsewhere. Such instances occur with various species that cannot possibly be charged with parasitic tendencies.

Nevertheless, parasitism is not unknown in North America and occurs in several species across the continent. The most common example nation-wide is the brown-headed cowbird, *Molothrus ater*, which lays its eggs in nests of more than 250 species and depends on the host species to hatch and care for its young. Among waterfowl, the red-headed duck, *Aythya americana*, frequently lays its eggs in the nests of other ducks and leaves the incubation and care of them to the nest owner.

Our American cuckoos are extremely poor nest builders. The nests are placed in coniferous and deciduous trees, or in bushes, and are well concealed by dense foliage. They consist of shallow, frail platforms composed of small rootlets, twigs, and a few dry leaves and bits of moss. The surface is lined with dry blossoms of flowering plants. These materials are loosely placed on the top of the little platform, which is so small that the extremities of the bird project on both sides. There is scarcely any depression to keep the eggs from rolling out. Some nests are so slightly built that the eggs can readily be seen through the bottom. Unless one parent remains on the nest during even a moderate windstorm, the eggs may easily roll out, and it is not a rare occurrence to find broken ones lying under the trees or bushes in which the nests are built.

With the exception of the ani, American cuckoos have moderately slender and decurved bills. Their tails are noticeably long and just after alighting, are raised and drooped slowly, or when their curiosity is aroused. Cuckoos, anis, and roadrunners all have unusual feet, with two toes facing forward and two backward. Toes one and four are turned backward, and toes two and three turned forward—an arrangement known as zygodactyl feet, well adapted for perching. In size, American cuckoos are larger than a robin, most between eleven and twelve inches in length. They are shy birds, and only by chance does one catch a glimpse of them as they fly swiftly from cover to cover.

As is the case with the roadrunner, the courtship feeding behavior pattern, in which the male offers food to the female, is a common practice throughout the Cuculiformes order.

The female's posture often simulates a young bird begging for food and may occur as part of the courtship period, during incubation, or even when there are young in the nest. It has been observed just before or during copulation in some cuckoos, and the behavior appears to occur primarily in species in which the sexes remain together throughout the breeding season.

Cuckoos are among the most useful of our American birds, mainly because of their fondness for destructive caterpillars, which constitute their principal food at times. Some cuckoos employ a peculiar method of consuming the hairy caterpillar by slowly moving it from end to end through the beak by a side-shifting motion of the mandibles, thus shearing off the prickly hairs before swallowing. A few of the hairs do escape this process and in time the inside of the bird's stomach becomes so felted with a mass of hairs and spines that it obstructs digestion. Then the bird merely sheds the entire stomach lining, meanwhile growing a new one. The cuckoo feeds freely on elderberries, grapes, mulberries, beetles, bugs, grasshoppers, and even small lizards and frogs.

Cuculidae are divided into three groups: roadrunners, which are ground dwellers; tree-dwelling cuckoos; and the anis, which live both on the ground and in trees. We have already described our roadrunners of the first group. We need only add here that a somewhat smaller species of roadrunner, *Geococcyx affinis*, with similar appearance and habits, occurs farther south in Mexico. Let us now consider the other two groups, starting with the tree-dwelling cuckoos.

The Yellow-Billed Cuckoo

The yellow-bill, *Coccyzus americanus,* is the most common cuckoo found in the United States. People call this slender bird the rain crow, and you may hear its prolonged song of hollow-sounding notes, ka, ka, ka, on cloudy summer days that threaten rain, and sometimes during the night.

The Bird

The yellow lower mandible and yellow eyelids distinguish this cuckoo from others. Eleven to thirteen inches in length, the yellow-bill shows white underparts, with olive to brown tones above, and outer tail feathers which shine black against large terminal white spots. The bird flies swiftly with remarkable ease and grace, and straight as a crow except when threading its way through the branches of trees. Streamlined to perfection, it glides noiselessly through the air with its long tail streaming out behind.

The Environment

The range of the yellow-billed cuckoo extends throughout temperate North America and the Caribbean region and into South and Central America. It is casual in Bermuda and accidental in western Europe. In winter, it migrates into Northern Columbia, Venezuela, and east to southeastern Brazil and eastern Argentina, and ranges south casually to central and west Argentina, Ecuador, and Columbia. In the United States it is the only cuckoo which nests west of the Rocky Mountains, and even there, it is not very common and is never found in the Rockies themselves.

The bird loves low trees and can be seen feeding among the foliage and terminal twigs. It prefers running water and seeks it out anywhere in its neighborhood. Originally, it haunted the native woodlands, but like many other species, it has learned to frequent the abodes of man where it is not molested and where it finds an abundant food supply in shade trees, orchards and gardens.

The yellow-billed, as we have said, is a migrant, and in the eastern and middle-western areas of the United States, where very common, it arrives from its southern wintering between the first and the middle of May, departing the middle or end of September. In the West, yellow-bills arrive in New Mexico and Arizona a bit later in May and also leave for the South in September.

The Diet

Like other cuckoos, the yellow-billed feeds on a great variety of insects but its favorite food is the hairy caterpillar, shunned by most other birds. In southern and central Arizona, this cuckoo arrives too late in the spring to prevent the tent caterpillar from completely denuding the willows and cotton-woods of the Santa Cruz and other rivers. When these trees put out new leaves, the birds eagerly consume the second infestation of caterpillars, which occurs in the summer rainy season. Yellow-bills are likewise helpful in preventing the defoliation of other forest trees.

Nesting and the Young

The yellow-billed breeds in areas of dense tree growth, and in the West, nests chiefly among willows and cotton-woods along the rivers and valleys of the Sonoran zone.

Three or four eggs comprise the usual clutch but as many as six to eight occur in a single nest, perhaps as the product of more than one female. The shell is smooth, without gloss, and the color varies from a uniform blue to a pale greenish-blue or greenish-yellow. The eggs are usually incubated by the female and take about fourteen days to hatch. They are laid on succeeding days so that young of different ages appear in the nest. Incubation is shared to some extent by both sexes, but the male shows little concern for the nestlings and changes his mate every year. If one approaches the nest, the mother bird may tumble to the ground from sheer fright, feign lameness, and trail her wings as she tries to entice the intruder away.

The newly-hatched chicks, almost naked, are black and greasy-looking creatures, and their sprouting quills make them even more repulsive. The young birds appear to be covered with tiny lead pencils, as feathers remain in their sheaths until they are nearly full grown, and when the sheaths break open, the down pushes out onto the tips of the incoming juvenile feathers. The transformation to fluffy feathers is very rapid, requiring only a few hours, and the birds do not leave their nest until fully feathered.

The Black-Billed Cuckoo

Unless you are a close observer, you may confuse the black-billed *Coccyzus erythropthalmus* with the yellow-billed cuckoo, so nearly do they resemble each other. The yellow lower mandible and yellow eyelids distinguish the latter, but much of what can be said of one species as to habits or food would apply to the other.

The Bird

The black-billed has red eyelids and a wholly black bill, as the name implies. It lacks the conspicuously black and white tail feathers and the cinnamon-rufous wing gloss of the yellow-bill, though size and shape of both cuckoos are alike. The song notes are also similar, except that the black-bills are softer, more liquid and not as deep-toned. This species, too, is sometimes called rain crow because it becomes noisier just before rain.

If anything, the black-billed is even swifter on the wing than the other cuckoo, but flies in the same direct, graceful manner. Again, it is the same shy recluse, haunting shady retreats among the dense foliage of woods. The bird is not afraid to frequent orchards and gardens in search of food, though it shuns any intimacy with human beings. One may hear its wandering voice, but seldom see more than a fleeting glimpse of its elegant form as it flies from tree to tree.

The Environment

The black-billed cuckoo is not as widely distributed as the yellow-billed, being confined in the breeding season to the northern half of the United States and southern Canada east of the Rocky Mountains. Within this range, it seems to be commoner northward and rarer southward than the other species. Where ranges overlap, both yellow- and black-billed cuckoos are often found together, although the black-billed is more of a woodland bird and more retiring.

The Diet

The food of the black- and yellow-billed cuckoos are similar, varying, in general, as the insects of the more northerly range may vary from those to the south.

Nesting and the Young

Nests are usually placed at low elevations, two to four feet above the ground in small trees or thickets. Some are flimsy affairs, but more substantially built than those of the yellow-billed. The birds construct their nests with twigs and dry stalks, lining them with both dry and fresh leaves. The black-billed have also been known to breed in colonies and are notoriously careless about laying in each other's nests. They may even deposit eggs in the nests of the wood peewee, cardinal, cedar waxwing, catbird, and wood-thrush. Two or three eggs make up the clutch. Aside from their deeper color, the eggs differ from those of the yellow-billed by their smaller size.

In defense of its eggs or young, the black-billed cuckoo is quite courageous and does not readily retreat. Both sexes are devoted parents, sharing the fourteen day incubation period and the care of the young. Though born blind and essentially naked, the black-billed chick is neither deaf nor dumb, and in proportion to its size is probably the strongest and most active nestling on the North American continent. Between seven to nine days old, with half its feathers unsheathed, the cuckoo suddenly leaves its nest and begins to climb among the branches overhead. If disturbed, these young cuckoos assume a hiding pose, standing upright, with neck stretched out, bill straight in the air, and they sit frozen in this position until the danger has passed. This climbing period lasts until they are able to fly.

The Mangrove and Maynard's Cuckoos

Finally, there remains to be mentioned two cuckoos, each very similar to the yellow-billed in appearance, diet and habits, and each found only in quite limited areas of southern Florida.

The mangrove cuckoo, *Coccyzus minor*, is a comparatively rare resident found in mangrove thickets along the Florida Keys and along the southwest coast to above Tampa Bay. They are usually outnumbered by the yellow-billed cuckoos, often seen side by side with them in low country. Their song notes are higher pitched and not as guttural and may be described as a rapidly uttered series of "kucks" suddenly changing to a deliberate "cow-cow-cow." Mangroves are summer residents from March to the end of November in the Bahamas and transient elsewhere in the West Indies. They winter in South America.

Maynard's cuckoo, a subspecies of the mangrove, lives throughout the forests near Cape Sable on Florida's southern tip and on the nearby islands as far as Key West. It may easily be mistaken for the yellow-billed cuckoo as tail markings are nearly the same. However, if clearly seen at close range, the grayish crown and the black area behind and below the eye are good field marks.

As a rule, this cuckoo is shy and through the winter rather silent, but as spring approaches it begins to utter singular cries and especially before rain is quite noisy like the yellow- and black-bills. Maynard fly faster than any of the American cuckoos and land suddenly without apparent lessening of speed. As soon as the feet touch a branch, a Maynard brakes itself by dropping its tail feathers like the wing flaps of an airplane.

This cuckoo lays eggs which are practically indistinguishable from those of the yellow-billed, and it raises two broods in a season. The bird eats caterpillars, spiders, moths, flies, and grasshoppers, but also, at times, a few small fruits and wild berries. Maynard range into the Bahamas, Cuba, northeastern South America, Central America, and Mexico.

The Groove-Billed Ani

So far, we have been describing American Cuculidae groups which have many similarities, but the third group, the anis, violates almost everything that has been held to characterize cuckoos.

The Bird

The groove-billed ani, *Crotophaga sulcirostris*, looks like a large blackbird, about fourteen inches long, with a grotesquely arched bill, and a tail that appears ready to fall off. Only at close range can you see the grooves in the thick bill. Observing the living birds, one would hardly suspect that anis were even related to the cuckoos, their appearance and habits are so different. The anis' notes are similar to the flickers' and the combination of "plee-co," rapidly repeated, sounds like "tijo, tijo" over and over again. Its ordinary conversational notes are a series of very liquid, contented bubblings and cluckings. A louder note, "chee-muy-o-chee-muy-o" is the alarm call and very distinctive.

The Environment

Anis are birds of open country, avoiding forested areas, and are one of the most conspicuous species in inhabited districts of humid coastal regions. Their favorite haunts include bushy pastures, orchards, fields and lawns, and clearings near human habitation. They like marshland as well as a dry hillside, and they are as numerous in extensive stands of sawgrass as in the Toloa Lagoon in Honduras. In semi-desert regions of the interior, they are the most common of birds, living among scattered cactii and acacias, but they thrive equally in the rankest vegetation of districts watered by twelve feet of rain annually. Though they occur at elevations as high as 5,000 feet, they prefer the lowlands.

In the United States, the groove-billed may be found in the lower Rio Grand Valley of Texas below 700 feet. It is a casual autumn straggler into southeastern Arizona, where there are records of sightings in the Chiricahua Mountains and at Fort Huachuca and Sabino Canyon Dam near Tucson. Anis do not normally come farther north than the Rio Yaqui in Sonora, Mexico, and even there it is a summer resident only. They are found east to Yucatan, south to Venezuela and west to Peru. A rare record was once made of this bird as far north as Red Wing, Minnesota.

The Diet

Anis' food consists largely of insects from the ground and among the foliage of bushes. They are often seen hunting grasshoppers and other creatures in high grass or tall weeds. They may leap a foot or so above the herbage to snatch up an insect which has tried to escape by flight. After the first heavy rain of each season, winged broods of termites swarm forth in countless millions, and one can watch the anis feeding like flycatchers, darting gracefully from low twigs and fences. However, in areas where the insects are epidemic, the birds can catch many without leaving their perches. To some extent, Anis also consume fruit and berries.

In Texas their apparent fondness for the company of cattle is due not only to the insects started up by the movements of the animals, but to the ticks and ectoparasites which they find on the animals' skin. The birds provide a sanitation service similar to that performed by the famous rhinoceros bird for its burly African companion. During the day, the anis may perch on the cattle as they feed, sometimes working along a cow's tail to clear it of insects to its extremity. Even at night when the animals are lying down, the anis cling to their backs.

Nesting and the Young

Anis remain together in small flocks from February to May, while other birds of the region are raising their broods, making anis among the latest birds to breed, usually in July and November. Nest building is very much a community affair and the large structures consist of a mass of sticks, twigs and grasses. Half a dozen birds may work in perfect harmony, operating in pairs, one bird fashioning the nest while its mate brings in material. Each pair prefers to work by itself at the nest, and if a second pair comes, the first pair quietly withdraws. On occasion, two females may work on the nest while the males bring them sticks for nesting material.

The normal set of eggs for each female in the community nest is three or four, and they are deposited in layers, each level covered by leaves. The birds of both sexes take turns in incubating the eggs, their shifts on the nest having no regular order or fixed duration. The eggs are a glaucous-blue and this color is overlaid and hidden by a thin, chalky deposit. As incubation advances and the birds turn the eggs, the white deposit is worn off until the blue is exposed.

The chicks, when hatched, are naked, blind, and black-skinned with no trace of feathers until about six days old. They are brooded by one parent for a week or so, and then other members of the flock join in the care of the nestlings.

Ani family members show a remarkable degree of affection and responsibility for each other. One of the young from a previous brood, nearly full grown, was observed to be a constant companion of his parents while they were busy with their second brood. He frequently perched on the rim of the nest, while one parent was incubating, and offered it food. When the young were hatched, this youngster helped in the feeding. He was also protective of them and in the absence of the parents, attempted to defend them alone.

The Smooth-billed Ani

The smooth-billed ani, *Crotophaga ani*, a curious tropical species of rare occurrence within the borders of the United States, may easily go unrecognized by bird watchers because, at a distance, they resemble common grackles.

The Bird

In length this bird measures between thirteen and fifteen inches. It may appear to be entirely black, but the feathers are actually margined with grayish-bronze in front and glossed with violet behind. The wings are small for the size of the bird, and the flight is not strong, consisting of a series of steady wing beats alternating with short sails. The smooth-billed can be distinguished from other black birds by the extraordinary bill, which is very deep at the base, with dorsal ridge higher and sharper than the groove-bills.

The notes of the smooth-bill consist of a wailing or whining whistle. It resembles the notes of the wood duck, varied by low clucking notes, while the call of the groove-billed is softer and higher in pitch. The smooth-billed travels on the ground in a most peculiar manner, as it hops and bounds about, lifting both feet together. The bird loves to sit on some low tree in the morning sun, basking with expanded wings, and will remain perfectly still for a long time in this position. Anis roost at night huddled closely on a branch like domestic fowl, and often bunch together in daytime during a rainstorm. They assemble in flocks that may contain from six to twenty or more individuals. The ani is polygamous and thus a number of females may accompany two or three males who take great care of them, uttering cries of alarm when they spot an intruder and driving the hens before them into cover.

The Environment

In the United States you may, if lucky, find this rather rare bird somewhere in the southern states from Louisiana to Florida, and north through the Carolinas, even as far as Pennsylvania. They live in the Bahamas, Haiti, Puerto Rico, and the Virgin Islands, ranging through the Lesser Antilles to eastern Brazil, and south to Argentina and Peru.

The Diet

Anis feed mainly in pasture lands but are found in cane fields and orange groves as well. Their food consists mainly of insects, fruit and berries. In seasons of abundance, the stomach becomes distended with caterpillars, moths, grasshoppers, and beetles, and it is amazing that such masses of food can be swallowed at one time. In the wake of brush fires, smooth-bills pick up roasted lizards, snails and insects. Like the groove-bills, they are called *tickbird* in some areas from their habit of eating the ticks infesting cattle.

Nesting and the Young

The nesting habits are most curious and interesting. As is the case with the groove-billed, all members of the flock participate in building the nests, which they place high in a tall tree, a clump of mistletoe, or cedar. The total number of eggs in each nest is determined by the number of birds in the company. Each female lays two blue eggs and again, like the groove-bills, deposits them in layers with leaves between. When the top layer is hatched and the young fledged, the leaves are scratched off and incubation continues with each descending layer until all eggs hatch. While most smooth-bills construct communal nests, sometimes single pairs build and incubate their nests alone, probably because they live in areas with fewer birds and thus lack the usual flocks to help them.

The young are hatched naked, covered with black skin and devoid of any trace of feathers. The eyes are tightly closed, but by the third day they open, and in six days the nestling can hop in and out of the nest and climb up the limbs of the tree. When half-grown they are fully feathered.

Thus do they live and eat and breed, those American cousins of the roadrunner, those two other groups of Cuculidae: the yellow-billed, black-billed, mangrove and Maynard cuckoos, as well as our strange birds, the grooved- and smooth-billed anis. It would be difficult to find any classification of birds more remarkable and fascinating than the Cuculidae, of which the roadrunner is doubtless the most amazing.

Chapter Five
THE PAISANO'S PLACE IN NATURE

Now that we have described the roadrunner and his habits, along with his relatives, it is essential that we attempt to estimate the role he plays in the environment and his contribution to the balance of nature.

Very few of my friends or neighbors are neutral on the subject of roadrunners. Some hate the bird because of bad reports or have themselves seen him act as a predator. Others, usually with more experience, hail him as a friend and delightful member of the bird world. Which attitude is closer to reality?

In the Southwest, the roadrunner was once labeled a pest, accused of living on birds' eggs and nestlings—a belligerent, cocky individual and a holy terror to many forms of wildlife. Bird fanciers watching a nest of young develop only to have it cleaned out by some predator, blamed a roadrunner, rather than a rat or snake.

Quail hunters reported large numbers of roadrunners living in a quail habitat and claimed that the quail were being decimated by this ugly bird with the long, sharp beak. Such negative reports soon made game officials hostile to all roadrunners, and it was not long before the bird was persecuted throughout his range as a *quail destroyer*. Several states offered bounties for his extermination. In November 1907, when biologist William Hornaday came to Arizona, he was surprised by the scarcity of this bird. Throughout his journeys across the deserts, he saw only two roadrunners, one in the suburbs of Tucson and the other near the Sonoita oasis.

A decade later, H. C. Bryant of the University of California conducted a scientific survey with surprising results. One hundred roadrunners in close proximity of nesting quail were observed and their food habits were studied from both field observations and stomach examinations. Bryant discovered that grasshoppers constituted sixty-two percent of the stomach contents while other food included centipedes, scorpions and tarantulas. The reptilian contents were composed mostly of lizards, though part of a rattlesnake was found. There was no evidence of quail or their eggs, although Bryant noted two cactus wrens, an unidentified sparrow and a nestling meadowlark.

Observation of the roadrunner's activities in a quail habitat showed that they were catching not quail but the grasshoppers that the quail stirred up. Too close an approach to a quail cock precipitated an immediate attack from which the roadrunner ran. Insects comprised almost seventy-five percent of the stomach contents of the roadrunners examined. No quail whatever were found, but lizards, rats, mice, a tiny cottontail rabbit, two small birds, and a small amount of vegetable matter, consisting of sour berries, made up the other twenty-five percent.

The report concluded that even if, at times, roadrunners destroy a few young quail, there is no evidence to support the contention that roadrunners, in general, are customary predators of quail. The survey revealed not a single instance of a roadrunner having destroyed quail eggs. That they do destroy large numbers of snakes, rats and other rodents which are far more destructive to quail and quail eggs than the roadrunner, was amply confirmed.

The tide of prejudice began to turn. Bird lovers hailed the roadrunner as a courageous and valuable friend of man, doing an enormous amount of good in the world. One observer reported, "They eat incredible numbers of the very pests man wants to be rid of—grasshoppers, crickets, caterpillars, beetles, centipedes, mice, lizards, and most important of all snakes—lots of snakes."[1] States that had enacted roadrunner bounties repealed them, and then went further and enacted protective laws. New Mexico made the roadrunner its State bird.

It is true that the Cuculiformes order of birds—roadrunners, anis and other cuckoos—do parasitize or prey upon other bird species. But such depredations, when compared to the value of ridding us of some of our most destructive pests, which other species will not touch, more than balances the scales in favor of these birds. The roadrunner, in particular, deserves our protection.

One summer, a few years ago, Fred Snyder, who was then president of the Northern Arizona Audubon Society, wanted to provide sugar water for the numerous black-chinned hummingbirds that came to his home in Sedona. He placed feeders approximately a foot above the deck of his rear porch, which was about twelve feet above ground, and the black-chins swarmed around them each day. He was later surprised to see a roadrunner on his porch leap up to one of the feeders and grab a hovering hummer in his beak. The runner proceeded to knock it senseless on the floor and swallow it head first. In the following days when Snyder saw the roadrunner catch and consume several more, he took preventive action by placing the nectar feeders on metal arms two or three feet away from the porch and out of the runner's reach. This stopped the roadrunner's game, but another smart alec, a desert raccoon, then discovered the nectar and consumed it each night until Snyder put tacks along the bracket arms, and the feeders were finally safe for the black-chins.

When this incident was reported in the Audubon Society newsletter, one bird lover was outraged that Snyder had not killed the roadrunner and suggested that he resign as president. Snyder replied that he loved *all* birds and that the roadrunner had only been doing what was natural. Aside from any Darwinian considerations as to the roadrunner's part in natural selection, whereby the poorest hummingbirds disappeared while the most alert and agile survived, there was another, more important factor. How many hummingbirds did that same roadrunner save by eliminating snakes and rats that prey upon the eggs and nestlings of hummers? Fred Snyder did not resign.

At Tonto Creek, I have noted that Ruby and the other runners pay no attention to the many hummingbirds that hover about the feeder near Ruby's feeding rock. Actually, by placing his feeders only a foot above his deck, Snyder had created, inadvertently and with the best of intentions, a sort of trap where hummers were enticed in such numbers to a feeding point within easy grab of a roadrunner—a situation unlikely to occur in nature.

Juncos, sparrows, finches, cardinals, robins, bluebirds,

and towhees abound in Tonto Creek. In the summertime, some of the sparrows and juncos depart and are replaced by kinglets, wrens, orioles, chats, and various species of humming-birds. Throughout the past four years of close observation, we have seen roadrunners capture only three sparrows and two nestling brown towhees.

The numerous coveys of quail we enjoy throughout the year can be quite defiant towards the roadrunners. We had been warned that we could not enjoy both, that the road-runners would clean out the quail and during the nesting season, their chicks. So in wintertime, when as many as 100 quail come to our place daily, and on occasion, our road-runners, particularly Ruby, dash into their midst, scattering them, we have worried a little. But never once has Ruby pursued or captured any individual bird, and we can only conclude that for her this is some sort of game.

During the nesting season, we have also watched families of quail arrive to drink at our small water pond and, with some trepidation, held our breaths when a roadrunner arrived at the same time. But again, not once have we seen them pay the quail the slightest bit of attention. Even when quail with their chicks come to our yard to peck at the grain, while our roadrunners are arriving and departing in a hurry to carry away hamburger to their young, it is not the roadrunner who takes on the aggressive role. On the contrary, when Ruby or Rachel, heading for another handout, enter the yard on the trot and carelessly run through the gathered quail, the chicks immediately scatter for cover. The adult quail then launch a fierce attack on the roadrunners. On one occasion, the attack was so severe that Ruby ran from the yard and out of sight with angry quail close at her heels, their wings extended. After a few of these combat scenes, the roadrunners quickly learned to make wide detours or to come in from a different direction to avoid trouble. We no longer fear for quail or chicks, realizing they are more than capable of fending for themselves.

From what I have observed, roadrunners save more quail and their eggs than they consume. Would it not have been ironic if, by killing off the roadrunner to *save* the quail, we had succeeded only in diminishing their numbers by permitting rats, mice and snakes to multiply and destroy eggs and nestlings. As it is, this place now swarms with both quail and roadrunners. Obviously the runner does play a constructive role in our environment and is an essential element in the balance of nature in the American Southwest.

REFERENCES

Chapter One

1. Dobie, Frank J. *Roadrunner in Fact and Folklore*, p. 2.

Chapter Two

2. Bailey. *Birds of New Mexico,* p. 309.

Chapter Three

1. Bent, Arthur C. *Life Histories*, p. 42.
2. Ibid., p. 44.
3. Ibid., p. 45.

Chapter Five

1. Smith, G. T. *Birds of the Southwestern Deserts*, p. 29.

BIBLIOGRAPHY

Allen, Arthur A. *The Book of Bird Life.* Princeton, New Jersey: D. Van Nostrand Co., Inc., 1961.

Allen, Glover Morrill, *Birds and their Attributes.* New York: Dover Publications, Inc., 1962.

Audubon Society. *Field Guide to North American Birds (Western Region).* New York: Alfred A. Knopf, 1947.

Bailey, Florence Merriam, Cook, Brooks and Fuertes. *Birds of New Mexico.* Albuquerque: New Mexico Department of Game and Fish, 1928.

Bent, Arthur Cleveland. *Life Histories of North American Cuckoos, Goatsuckers, Hummingbirds, and Their Allies,* Part I. New York: Dover Publications, 1964.

Berger, Andrew J. *Bird Study.* New York: Dover Publications, Inc., 1971.

Blanchon, Neltje. *Bird Neighbors.* New York: Garden City Publishing Co., 1904.

Bryant, Harold C. "Habits and Food of the Roadrunner in California," in D. M. Gorsuch, *Arizona Wildlife: Report of U.S. Biological Survey,* October 1932.

Burton, Maurice, Dr., and Robert Burton, General Editors. *Funk and Wagnalls Wildlife Encyclopedia,* No. 5. New York, 1974.

Campbell, Elizabeth W. Crozer. *The Desert Was Home.* Los Angeles, California: Westernlore Press, 1961.

Chapman, Frank M. *Bird Life.* New York: D. Appleton & Co., 1901.

Clement, Roland C. *American Birds.* New York: Bantam Books, 1973.

Dobie, J. Frank. "The Roadrunner In Fact and Folklore," in *Arizona Highways,* Phoenix, Arizona: May 1968, pp. 2-11.

Douglas, Virginia. "A Run of Roadrunners," in *Arizona Magazine,* Phoenix, Arizona: Arizona Republic Newspaper, January 6, 1980, pp. 28-31.

Eliot, Willard Ayres. *Birds of the Pacific Coast.* New York: G. P. Putnam, 1923.

Hornaday, William T. *The American Natural History,* Vols. II & III. New York: Charles Scribner & Sons, 1914.

————. *Campfires on Desert and Lava.* New York: Charles Scribner & Sons, 1908.

Jaeger, Edmund C. *The California Deserts*. Stanford, California: Stanford University Press, 1933.

————. *Desert Wildlife*. Stanford, California: Stanford University Press, 1950.

Knowlton, Frank H., F. A. Lucas and Robert Ridgeway. *Birds of the World*. New York: Henry Holt, 1909.

Krutch, Joseph Wood. *The Voice of the Desert*. New York: William Sloane, 1954.

Ligon, J. Stokley, *New Mexico Birds*. Albuquerque, New Mexico: University of New Mexico Press, 1961.

McGraw-Hill, "Life in Parched Lands," (a film of the road-runner versus a rattlesnake).

Pearson, Gilbert T., editor. *Birds of America*. New York: Garden City Publishing Co., 1936.

Phillips, Allan, Joe Marshall and Gale Monson. *The Birds of Arizona*. Tucson, Arizona: University of Arizona Press, 1964.

Rigby, Douglas. *Desert Happy*. New York: J. B. Lippencott Co., 1957.

Robbins, Chandler S., Bertel, Bruun and Hubert S. Zim. *Birds of North America, A Guide to Field Identification*. Golden Press, 1966.

Schaldach, William J. *Path to Enchantment: An Artist in the Sonoran Desert*. New York: MacMillan Press, 1963.

Sheehey, Katherine. "Clown of the Desert," in *Desert Magazine of the Southwest*. August, 1977, pp. 40-41.

Smith, Gusse Thomas. *Birds of the Southwestern Desert*. Scottsdale, Arizona: Doubleshoe Publishers, 1941.

Stokes, Frederick A. *The Charm of Birds*. London: Vicount Grey, 1927.

VanDyke, John C. *The Desert – Further Studies in Natural Appearances*. New York: Charles Scribner & Sons, 1901.

Wallace, George J. *An Introduction to Ornithology*. New York: The MacMillan Company, 1955.

Welles, Philip, *Meet the Southwest Deserts*. Tucson, Arizona: Dale Stuart King, Publisher, 1960.

Welty, Joel Carl. *The Life of Birds*. New York: Alfred A. Knopf, 1963.

Whitson, Martha A. "The Roadrunner – Clown of the Desert," in *National Geographic*, May, 1983, pp. 695-702.